Gypsy Mercer

Virgo Unbound

Gypsy Mercer

Gypsy Mercer

Virgo Unbound
Copyright © 2021 *by Gypsy Mercer*

Editor: Ashley Jane

Cover Artwork via Design Bundles

All rights reserved. No part of this publication may be reproduced, distributed, or transmitted in any form or by any means, without prior written permission.

Author's Note: This is a work of fiction. Names, characters, places and incidents are a product of the author's imagination. Any resemblance to actual people, living or dead, or actual events is purely coincidental.

Virgo Unbound/Gypsy Mercer ~ First Edition
ISBN: 978-1928877066

Dedication

To the one missing from me

"Je t'aime et tu me manques"

My love always

Gypsy

Gypsy Mercer

Other books by Gypsy Mercer

Into the Fire: Musings of a Gypsy Soul

(2018)

Surviving the Storm: Musings of a Gypsy Soul

(2019)

Falling Rain: Musings of a Gypsy Soul

(2020)

The Lone Wolf

(2020)

FOREWORD

If you are a follower of Gypsy Mercer and have read her previous books, you are in for a soul-drenching, mystical experience. In this book, *Virgo Unbound*, the author has delved deep, fathoms below her poetic surface, and has curated a treasure trove of personal poetry.

Her creations have long touched hearts across social media, and her confessional style of heart-gripping prose is one of my favorite daily reads. But, I have to say that this book was unexpected in that I could feel a more personal connection to the author.

You are granted a front row seat as you watch a soul begin to unravel the binds that dare to encapsulate and strangle the passion that's been forced to lie dormant. The author shows us her strength as she unleashes and builds anew. There is freedom that comes from letting go, from drawing boundaries and enforcing them, and you feel the release page after page.

Gypsy Mercer

Gypsy's words serve as a reminder that we all need to look below the surface and swim the depths of our inner most desires. Too often, we backstroke with the methodical current of the day while our passions simmer untapped below. Perhaps, after reading this book, you will be tempted to explore the crevices and unbind your inner Virgo.

From one Virgo to another... I know I am inspired.

Alfa Holden
Bestselling Author of *I Find You in the Darkness, I Needed a Viking, She Wears Pain Like Diamonds,* and 5 other poetry books

VIRGO

My Virgo to your Sagittarius
Earth and Fire
My intensity
Your passion
You ignited a flame
Too hot to contain

Gypsy Mercer

VENUS IN VIRGO

Venus in Virgo
Feminine
Sensual
Pleases her mate
Is his heart's desire
Never demanding
    Never assuming
Freely gives that which pleases her
Wary and watchful
    Lest you make a mistake
Rewards respect with loyalty
Teach her to laugh
She needs freedom
    And trust
To become her best self
She is for your growth
    And your pruning
The gentle breeze that satisfies
    Your dreams
Should she leave
She will leave a vacuum
That can never be filled

MERCURY IN VIRGO

Mercurial Virgo
    Smart
    Beautiful
    Creative
    Shy

Never rude
    Nor dishonest
    Nor naïve

Always practical
Always faithful
Always honorable
Always truthful

A refined taste
    To be explored

Gypsy Mercer

<u>DAWN</u>

Waiting for dawn to break
The darkness fades to light
The monsters
The angels too
Lie in wait for night
   To fill our dreams
   To taint our day
   To help us find our way

MADNESS

I wonder
When your madness passes
Will there still
    Be room for me
When twilight sets in
Will I still have a starring role
    Or fade to pastel hues
To be forgotten
Until the next full moon

Gypsy Mercer

SOLACE

He seeks out the lonely

Offering solace

Listening

Caring

A friendship born of need

So little

So right

So needed

So everything

SMOLDER

If you have no passion
    For life
    For me
Stay away
My flame
Burns brightly
Consuming mediocrity
Melting the ordinary
Do not try to douse
My fire
It may smolder
But rise again
It will spread
Even further
This time

Gypsy Mercer

HEARTBREAK

Do not test me
I may fail
Your expectations are many
My response limited
To what I am willing
    To show you
My waters run deep
Colored by experiences
I will not share
If telling you
    If showing you
Is insufficient
We both lose
And that is heartbreak

Virgo Unbound

YOU

In the misty morning light
I find you
My dreams a reality
Your body next to mine
Your smile so divine
You have captured my heart
My thoughts always spring to you
You are my hopes and dreams
Come to life
The one I knew
Was waiting for me
And I for you
You nourish my soul
And fill my life with love
Making me whole

Gypsy Mercer

LAUGHING

If I give you my heart
Will you teach me
To love again

If I give you my love
Will you teach me
To laugh again

If I give you my laughter
Will you help me
Find my words again

I GIVE YOU ME

You know my secrets
You know my lies
My guard does not function
Around you
My walls have crumbled
My innocence
My guilt
Transparent before you
Baring all
A virgin to your love
I give you
Me

Gypsy Mercer

<u>A NEW YEAR</u>

Breaking dawn
A new year
Second chances
New beginnings
Our love
Continues
To grow
Giving us strength
And renewed magic

FATE

We have more past
    Than future
We do not have to hurry
    Anymore
It is all about us
    In the moment
Making memories
    To take
Into our tomorrows
    After tears have fled
Finding us alone
    In our own head
Reliving the best
    Forgetting the rest

Gypsy Mercer

DANDELIONS

I turn the page
Expecting dandelions
Wispy and free
Traveling
I know not where

I see daffodils instead
Heralding spring
And new beginnings
Only to find
They are mired in the past
A past that accepts
Only you
Once again

HALF-MEASURES

Living life by half-measures
Fearing the fall
Is not living
It is isolation
While our body plays
Our heart constrained
Conflicted and bleeding
For the freedom
It deserves
To freefall
Without a net
Without fear

Gypsy Mercer

<u>TINDER</u>

I have waited for you
Years and days and hours
We had the air
    Heat
    Tinder
Combustion was assured
Blue flames spiked
Dancing to the rhythm
    Of our heartbeat
But rain doused our fire
Leaving smoldering ruins
Yet it lived
    In our hearts
    In our memories
Refusing to die
We stoked the fire
And flame was reborn
Why did we wait so long
To finally live our love

DEMAND

You reacted to my weakness
    And now you pay
What began as love
    Turned to habit
    Turned to assumption
I never meant it so
My inconsistencies
Became your demand
Love faltered
Dying of your expectancy

Gypsy Mercer

MIST

She is all mist
    And magic
Never quite strong enough
    To stay
    To commit
Always hesitant
Thus falling from the sky
Into the fire and ash
Of broken dreams

SIRENS

Waves peak
    And crash
To a melody christened by sirens
The symphony of song and sea
Claim another soul
    To her bosom
Leaving heartbroken maidens
    To mourn the tides
That ever flow
Back from whence they came

Gypsy Mercer

THE MOON

I call
You answer
But never call
Your voice so full of promise
Falls flat in the follow through
Days turn to weeks
Hoping
This time my phone will ring

Am I safely in yesteryear
Only thought of
    When you hear my voice
Am I a smoldering passion
    Waiting to reignite
A dark corridor
Of your soul
When the moon is right

PUSHING

When I push you away
You must pull me back in
Because I need you most
    When I run away
You must find me
    Because I am scared
As many times
As it takes
Until I stop pushing
    And running
    And believe
You are for keeps

Gypsy Mercer

<u>I FORGOT</u>

Momentarily I forgot
    Who you are
    What you are
Then I remembered
What a foolish mistake
It does not suit to forget
It is dangerous and dark
    If I lose my footing
It is game set match
I was lulled into complacency
You were simply hibernating
Gathering your strength
What a fool I was to blink
My eyes are clear now
And focused on you

TRUST

You are the man
I have always wanted
The details were unclear
But the feelings were not
You led me to paths
I have never explored
With you as my guide
I do not hesitate
That scares me most of all
My acceptance of you
My complete trust in you
My dismissal of fear
And your confidence

Gypsy Mercer

SEASONS

In what season will you claim me
White hair impersonating early winter
Will your love take away the chill
Descending upon my heart
Covering the embers of lost loves
What propels your visit now
When the years take a sharp decline
Will love simply be a convenience
Born of loneliness or proximity
Or will it be the love long awaited
Will you give the best or the rest
I will not hold back
My love will be fiery
My love will be serene
We will ride an emotional ladder
To capture a lifetime of waiting
Before we slip into the night
And live perpetual dreams

LEAVE

I wish you to vacate my prison
The walls keep me safe
    And free
You were not meant to get this close
You crowd my thoughts
    My actions
You limit my imagination
As I fight for space
    To breathe
It is not love
I sought from you
Merely transient companionship
You are not welcome
In my world
Leave me in peace

Gypsy Mercer

CHERISH

This time I will leave
Sweet words and promises
    Will not hold me
Second chances
Second dances
I grew so tired
    Waiting for you
To accept me
As I am
    In my madness
    In my sadness
    In my glee
    In my plea to be free
        Of your sorcery
Your games
Are for someone new
I need someone
Who will cherish
    And honor me
Who will love me
    In spite of me being me

REMEMBERING

It has been so long
Since I felt the sweetness of love
The promise of forever
The all-consuming need
My doors are rusted shut
    The hinges inoperable
But my mind remembers
The complete surrender
    Of my soul
I miss the euphoria of love
    With each passing hour
The days are long
The nights are longer
I pray

Gypsy Mercer

SADNESS *(Collaboration with The Ruined Man)*

I wear a sadness
I do not share
Though my eyes sparkle
The window is closed

I wear a pain
I do not share
Though my heart is bleeding
The drops are silent

Clouds hide the light
Rain masks the tears
Remembering
A love that died
Fading
Before its time

VINE

Did you live before him
Really live and breathe
Did he bring you to life
Examining every petal
Holding it up to the sun
Trailing it across his cheek
Until all its beauty
Was absorbed by his heart
Did your sweet nectar
Fuel his imagination
    His passion
Only to die on the vine
Used and lonely
Failing the test of time

Gypsy Mercer

<u>SANITY</u>

Have you made decisions
Putting someone else
Above you
These are the hardest
    To live through
    To forget
In saner moments
When the moon is not full
Would you do it again

PATHS

Some journeys are alone
Yet not lonely
Some open gates
Some offer detours
Some bring happiness
Some do not
I open my gate to you
To share my journey
With all its peace
    And chaos
A convergence
Of heart and soul
Known to angels
    And demons alike

Gypsy Mercer

SUMMER STORM

You are the approaching summer storm
    Cleansing and pure
You are my bonfire
    Fury and light
You are the thunder
    That restarts my heartbeat
You are the ocean's gentle caress
You are the cool on a forest path
You are the moon that illuminates
    My way
        And shapes my dreams
You are all that feeds my soul
    Opening it to love
        Once more

LET ME GO

Let me go free
To run with the wolves
Following my instincts
Protecting my flank
Let me love as though
You never broke my heart
Let me be free
To find my smile
To welcome a new man
Who erases the doubts
You buried in my head
Let me experience
A first kiss
Passionate enough
To forget our last
Then and only then
Will I be truly free
To move on

Gypsy Mercer

INDESTRUCTIBLE

I will not live
In the shadows
I shine too brightly in the sun
I am your trenchant weapon
Front and center
Or
Side by side
I reinforce your power
I underscore your strength
United we are indestructible
As warriors are meant to be
Whom even the gods fear
Once the gauntlet is thrown

ACCEPTANCE

The walls are steel
They shield me
I see life as a play
And wonder at my role
    People pleasing
    Contrite
From the outside looking in
Acting like me
But the mirror has no reflection
The ground rumbles
And is steep
I know the path
Is across a bridge
Marking acceptance
Maybe I am too vain
To find this key
And will forever
Be an audience to my life

Gypsy Mercer

ALIVE

You stand tall
    And alone
Watching life's merriment
Happy for those included
Stoic
Yet your heart burns
    Wanting to play
Believing your time has passed
Not willing to gamble your heart
    Fractured by deceit
    And complacency
Knowing your heart is on fire
Waiting for air to breathe
Allowing Lady Love
To kiss you alive

VALKYRIE

The Valkyrie rides Aragorn again
In tune with the pounding rain
Hooves thundering on the hard soil
Racing to a battle
    She will surely claim
She fears not defeat
    But her blood boils
In a primal dance
Raging for release
Against one
She considers equal

Gypsy Mercer

GONE

Why am I able to say the things
That would bring you closer
    In my head
Long after you are gone
Why do I remember the best stories
    Or jokes
Long after your laughter is done
Why must I continually be
Ten paces behind your reality
Begging you to stay
Yet when you are near
All I feel is love

SILENCE

In silence

I find myself

Alone

But complete

Taught myself love

Allowing me

To chase shadows

Befriending my ghosts

Hidden in the mind spring

Of my unconscious

I wander through clarity

To find my essence

And ease my mind

Before it hides

Once more

Gypsy Mercer

<u>STRONG MEN</u>

What happened to the strong men
Who fought for what they believed in
Who did not play it safe
Who followed their heart
Who thought original thoughts
Who felt other people's joy
Who walked the beach alone
Who held your hand
Who go the extra mile
Who kiss your forehead
Who cry at inequity
Who snuggle a dog
Who will love me without preamble
Demanding the best of me?

BREAK

Sometimes the weight

Stops me in my tracks

Sometimes I must remember

What I chose to forget

Do I go

Do I stay

Both

Break my heart

Leaving me teetering

At the precipice

Of confusion

And delusion

As the rocks slide

Gypsy Mercer

<u>MISS YOU</u>

He was a habit
I kept returning to
Never quite enough to keep me
    But enough to hold me
When loneliness
    And desire
Rear their head
Saying
I do not want to be alone
    And the cycle repeats
One day
You will not let me return
And I will miss you so

MIDNIGHT

Not midnight
That is too ordinary
We will wait
A full moon
To light our way
Following our own compass
True north
Where stars promise fulfillment
Granting wishes
We believe too impossible
To speak or dream
Much less to live
Yet too real to doubt
And daylight cannot shatter

Gypsy Mercer

ERASE

You did not need to erase him
    From your life
He will forever be in your heart
    His laughter
    The twinkle in his eyes
    The strength to hold you
    The courage to love you
These will never be forgotten
You were a team
Fighting life's battles
Emerging victorious
Amidst changing tides
    Threatening to topple you
The battle ended
He turned left
You turned right
The memory remains

TODAY

I thought of you today
It has been years
And I found you
You are doing well
You appear happy
That made me sad
Why do I wear your scars
While you run free
To hurt
Or to destroy
Or take the innocence
From so many
My hope for you
Is that you too wear
Someone's disrespect
And disregard
Deep inside

Gypsy Mercer

TIME

You are my secret place

Where I come alive

My emotions are unguarded

My imagination limitless

My fears nonexistent

My joy complete

You are my reality

Breaking through time

Loving me

As much as I love you

A continuous loop

Without end

LOSS

I loved you
And I hated me
    For my weakness
You felt the same
It took years
    To recognize the bravery
    Of opening my heart to you
You felt the same
Unfortunately
    We learned too late
    To save us
What a loss
What a horrible loss

Gypsy Mercer

WAITING

I wait for you to notice me
Your after thoughts
Are not enough
To feel this hungry heart
You have the ability
To start a fire
That will outshine the sun
So intense the moon
Will be in shadows
And smiles will blind

BACK TO YOU

I search for words
    The right words
        The powerful words
To give you strength
    To give you purpose
        To give you answers
I want the world to renew for you
    I want your dreams to come true
        I want the love you pursue
To be about me and you

Gypsy Mercer

HEAVEN

The years wash over me
My spark hides
I still dream
    Of perfection
I abhor mediocrity
I still demand
    Your best
And offer you mine
Gentler love
    Is still passionate
More subtle in the giving
Fine honed by experience
That meets you
In the all consuming
Rise to heaven
Breathing love once again

LONELINESS

Time is running out
We waited too long
To move forward
Survival was inherent in the games
We did not know we played
We were cautious
Afraid of commitment
Waiting for a sign
In time to prevent our fall
We wasted time
We withheld love
The love we needed
To end our loneliness
And let love in

Gypsy Mercer

ALONE

He walked into the room
GQ down to his pocket square
Not necessarily tall
Yet he dominated the room
Jet black hair
Eyes so green
They seemed surreal
He is aware of his power
    To tease your imagination
    To alter your perception
    To rule your world
The gentle lift of his lips
As he nears
Sharing my fantasy
Of hours uninterrupted
By the realities of the world

Virgo Unbound

REMEMBER

I am not here
To help you forget
Rather the opposite
I want to build memories
    Of the sweetest
Most passionate kiss
The feel of my skin
    When goose bumps erupt
    And our bodies are slick
My purr at your pleasure
The catch in my breath
The whispers in my throat
    My touch
    My smell
And how I interrupt your sleep
    Your concentration
    Your thoughts

Gypsy Mercer

TRANSCENDENCE

You belong to me
I love you in ways
Others would never dare
I read your mind
    Answer your needs
        Before you know they exist
I do not own you
    But you cannot leave
Our feelings so surreal
    Sublime in their delicacy
Intangible but potent
And I belong to you
Your love stirs my soul
    Takes me places only we can be
Full circle transcendence
    Into the ethereal mist

RIPOSTE

I was ready to go
The fury of our words
Sliced deeply
We knew just where to aim
To inflict the most pain
I felt it as I dealt it
I bled from your riposte
I lunge
You parry
Neither surrender
Neither win
Both lose
This dance of death
The loss of love

Gypsy Mercer

ADORATION

Once you held my heart
I rose to your sunshine
And slept at your feet
You did not love me
You succumbed to adoration
From others
Not recognizing the purity
Of my gift to you
You simply bathed in my glory
Your madness
    Was compelling
I could not walk away
I had no will of my own
My need to please you
    Was absolute

MAYBE

I want to snap my fingers
    And be in love
Maybe we were late bloomers
    In the love game
Maybe we never found
    The right one
        And settled
Rather than be alone
Maybe we missed it
    In our complacency
Maybe we just did not
    Recognize it
Maybe we found it
    And foolishly threw it away
Maybe waiting for the right one
    And the right time
Is now

Gypsy Mercer

CLOSE THE DOOR

Close the door

Throw away the keys

Let there be just you and me

    Laughing

    Crying

    Loving

Without the shields

Without the weapons

You and I left on the other side

ENOUGH

I am afraid
Of loving you
Too much
I feel vulnerable
Subject to heartbreak
    At a mere frown
    A raised eyebrow
    A hesitation
I am unable to move
Past this
    Please love me enough
    Hold me tight enough
    Be strong enough
To stay

Gypsy Mercer

TIDE

The ebbing tide
Graceful in its exit
Silently uncovering gems
Once lost
A wonderland of imagination
Grows by the inch
    Reflections
    Deflections
The buried past
    Questions
    Insight
    Answers
Forever changed
Awaiting rebirth

DREAM

I want to feel your touch
Caressing my soul
Bringing me back to life
Opening my eyes
Warming my heart
Filling me with love
Hope and promise
Secure in your embrace
A dream so surreal
I die of rapture
In your arms
Rather than wake

Gypsy Mercer

<u>TEARS</u>

We have changed
Carefree days
Passionate nights
Teased our imagination
Do you remember
When I was the one
That completed you
Yet you left
In a hazy streak of blue
Followed by darkness
Extinguishing my light
My tears formed a river
Cascading down
Into a swirl of chaos
Hell bent on destruction

Virgo Unbound

KISS

Will I ever love again
Or is my story over
Cast in shadows
And daydreams
Will my body feel
A welcoming embrace
Will my lips taste
A passionate kiss
Will my pulse race again
Must I be content
Reliving old loves
Imagining different
Scenarios and
Outcomes
Where do I use up
This love
I have left
Inside of me
If this is all there is

Gypsy Mercer

TIMING

Your timing
Is what made you special
My heart was broken
You found a way in
You set up house
You made a home
The once barren wasteland
Flowed with your love
Flowers began to bloom
Filling me with such tenderness
I pray it is enough
To burn the memories
That still haunt me

SAFE

I am immune to it
The memories
The emotions
Cut off from the past
Whole
I closed the door
Locked and bolted
The entrance
You cannot touch me
I am safe
Until you knock
And I let you in

Gypsy Mercer

INSTEAD

My heart is more vulnerable
Than my body
So I give it to you instead

Truth is born of adversity
Fine-tuned by lies
Emerging victorious
Albeit a bit bloody

Strength is also born of adversity
Building foundations
Some crumbling like sand
Some lasting throughout time
Scars born
And worn
With pride
And deliverance

EXHALE

The catch in your voice
The exhale in mine
Tells us
We are perfect
Together
No space between you and me
When we touch
Our bodies
Our spirits
Our hearts
Our souls
Combine as one
There is no greater union
Than when we melt
Into each other

Gypsy Mercer

STILL

Why does it always come back
    To me and you
The connection so real
Separate
Always trying to merge
Knowing our place
Is together
Still Trying
Still missing
Still you

THUNDER

A council of clouds
Waiting for the rain to pass
Thunderbolts full of anger
Engaged in fiery warfare
Fighting the invisible foe
Raised swords striking
Silently illuminating the sky
The steel of rage
Buried deep into the enemy
Stealthily withdrawing
Homeward bound
Once again victorious

Gypsy Mercer

CAPTURED

He was ever so polite

He was so sincere

Always complimentary

Forever smiling

With sparkling blue eyes

And cleft chin

He was my confidant

He played me like a kitten

With a ball of yarn

Drawing me in

Bit by bit

It was so natural

Lost in love

Captured

Not recognizing his game

LESSONS

You learned the lesson well
He said
After I responded
Just like he would
Why does he not appreciate
How well I learned
The game
When I win

Gypsy Mercer

<u>ONE</u>

I am not meant to follow

But you may walk beside me

My trust in you is absolute

Our hearts

Our lives

Depend on it

We are mated for life

We are one

We are Alpha

REGRET

I am alone in a forest
Of regret
I should have believed
In us
Ridding the doubt
From my thoughts
I could have tried harder
To understand
Your feelings
I should have believed in you

Gypsy Mercer

TOGETHER

You may lead

And I may follow

Protecting our flank

We are a team

We know our strengths

Together

We know them

Apart

We are undefeatable

Acting as one

FLAME

You are extraordinary
Kind and loving
But it is not enough
To hold me
I need fire
A flame to consume me
To be reborn
In every kiss
Every Embrace
A flame
That raises me
Higher than love
I wanted you to be
Enough
For my hungry soul

Gypsy Mercer

SLOW DANCE

Slow dancing with a ghost
Of what should have been
On yesterday's arm
Full of charm
Swaying to a memory
Tarnished by time
The witching hour near
Her prince to disappear
Unanswered questions
In his wake
Insuring heartbreak

REGRET

When it is quiet
My thoughts return to you
Remembering
The laughter
The love
We shared
And wishing
It never ended
My eyes still spill
With regret

Gypsy Mercer

<u>FIRE</u>

Play with my fire

And you will be burned

Ignite my fire

Fan my embers

Embrace my flame

And we will burn together

An eternal flame

The gods will envy

DENOUEMENT

The ultimate denouement
Crippling in its finality
Strangers
Where once was love
The cruelest edge of the sword
Belying our truth
Denying
Defiling
Our connection

Gypsy Mercer

WAR

We loved with such passion

We fought with such conviction

Together or apart

Our love so deep we wept when parting

Our wars drew nothing but defeat

I could not bear the pain

Of staying

Of leaving

I lost myself

In the battle

Choosing to save you

Sacrificing me

DISCOVERING LOVE

Falling rain reminds me of you
Far from sadness
Rather a lost day in the woods
Sheltered
The warmth of your body
Warding off the chill
Laughter
Snuggles
Dreams
Awakening me
Discovering love

Gypsy Mercer

ECHO

I want you at my side

We are stronger together

My mind seeks you

My heart holds you

Listen

Listen for my melancholy howl

Echoing across the miles

Listen to the mournful chords

Remind you

I love you

I miss you

Hurry home

FREEDOM

My heart
As light as the darkest night
Knowing what comes next
You told me you loved me
Knowing what to expect
How can I rush these words
When my soul is still filled
With him
My heart is straining
Against the chains that bind
Me to him
As it aches
For freedom
To love you too

Gypsy Mercer

DOUBT

He asked if I was happy
    He needed validation
I said yes
I did not tell him
My fear of losing myself
    In him
Of valuing him
    Over me
Of agreeing
    When I disagreed
Of following
    Not leading
Of falling
    Not floating
Of doubting
    Not believing
Yet I smiled
And kissed his lips
Wondering why he asked

SUNDAY MORNINGS

Sunday mornings
Wrapped in your love
Laughter
Dreams and plans
Breakfast in bed
Funny papers
Pillow fights
Dressed
You are gone
The memories remain
Of perfect days

Gypsy Mercer

TOGETHER

I was young
You were experienced
You knew
I soon would be
I was a woman
You made me yours
You drew me in
I had no choice
Your eyes were on fire
Your Alpha sensed mine
Though hidden
Together
We lit the sky

GRACE

You were always grace
Under fire
Hiding under a mask
Of contempt
Unreadable
Poised
Until
She tempted your heart
Ignoring her
Laughing at her
Did not help
Her pull was too strong
Losing
Never felt so right

Gypsy Mercer

WOLF MOON

Tonight

A full moon

The Wolf Moon

I will howl

From every timbre of my body

Pledging my love

For you

And you alone

Find me my Alpha

My love

I await

I am ready

APOLOGY

My apology
Although forthcoming
Was not sufficient
To your needs
I did not afford you
The attention you deserved
Your heart full of concern
My thoughts scattered
Unable to focus
I failed you
I am sorry
You are worth
More
Than I had to give

Gypsy Mercer

A KISS

A kiss

Lips meeting

Tasting

Gently opening

Giving access to so much more

Our tongues do foreplay

A medley of sensation

Turning thrusts into

Sword play to tease

Now longer

Now deeper

Breaths shorten

Body Awakened

CARDINAL

Eight cardinals came calling
Mesmerizing in opulent red
Hopping
Flying low
I stood transfixed
As their performance ensued
Hypnotized by their dance
They were startled
By an unhuman sound
And scattered
Two flew into my window
Bouncing off
Realizing
I could not protect them
From the fears in their mind

Gypsy Mercer

SHALLOWS

I do not play well in the shallows
My thoughts run too deep
I need shadows
Along with clarity
To paint a clear picture
Of what was
What is meant to be
I must immerse my body
And swim free of chaos
Arriving on the beach
Of reality

ABANDON

I love you with abandon

No hesitation

No remorse

Do not believe it is free

There is always a cost

You always pay

For perfection

I will take your heart

Ensnare your soul

Capture your imagination

Until all senses

Lead to me

Only then

Will I truly be yours

As you are mine

Gypsy Mercer

BECAUSE OF YOU

Because of you
    I believe in myself
Because of you
    My walls came down
Because of you
    I smiled once more
Because of you
    I believed in us
Because of you
    I cried
As your knife
Plunged deeply
Into my heart
Forever tainting love

MY ALPHA

Alpha in my own right
I search for my Alpha
Amongst sheep
What fool I am
To think you would
Be found there
You stand tall
All knowing
Confident
Awaiting your Alpha
To make herself known
A perfect fit
Beside you

Gypsy Mercer

POWER

I search for you
Behind every door
And I find you
Exactly where I left you
Last time
Bold and beautiful
Hungry for me
In the witching hour
Arms wrapped around me
Tasting my fire
Screaming for heaven
Blanketed in sin
You know your power

Virgo Unbound

WAITING

I waited
After the door closed
Day turned to night
Until I no longer believed
Then began again
Flexing my heart muscles
Smiling with the sun
Inhaling moonlight
Knowing
You are the one
I have waited for

Gypsy Mercer

TIME

It is but a glimmer
Of a dream
A fantasy
From a lifetime ago
I see you
Knowing your words
Your moves
Your love
Answering my prayers
In flesh and blood
Real this time

GAMES

You were the "it" man

Sophistication

Class

Sexy

Passionate

Romantic

Why did I feel

Like another chapter

An exercise

A target

When did you realize

Two can play

This game

Gypsy Mercer

SILENCE

Approaching quietly

Moving with the wind

Silently stalking my prey

Watching every move

Sensing hesitation

As you feel danger

Remaining calm

Contemplating escape

Relaxing

Recognizing my departure

OLD MOVIES

Sometimes
I feel an acute pain
In my heart
You appear in my thoughts
When my defenses are down
Just when I am sure
You are no longer
Hiding in my soul
You take up residence
Like old movies
Relived again
Making lonely nights
Happy again
In my dreams

Gypsy Mercer

GHOSTS

I do not want to remember

Love

I would rather live in

Half-measures

Diluted wines

Faded jeans

Unfinished books

The road most traveled

Is filled with potholes

Give me the open highway

No more heart and soul

No more searing pain

Nor the loneliness that follows

Let me live in the shadows

Befriending ghosts

RAIN

His reign is ending
I watched it fall
The skies opened
Spraying a fine mist
Of promises made
In the heat of the night
Never meant for daylight
The man stands tall
His woman no more
Than a shadow
Of dreams ended
Once strong
Bending not breaking
Taking his last bow
As the tears fall
His rain is ending
I saw it fall

Gypsy Mercer

BLINDED

I loved you

Proved it in my actions

And my words

Our laughter was playful

Our conversations deep

I respected you

Even when I did not understand

I followed

Even when you were lost

I was blinded

By your witchery

I did not expect a knife

In my back

As a thank you

And goodbye

MISSING PIECE

Love makes and breaks
Soulmates search
Souls evolve as does love
Soulmates find us
Sometimes it is
    The right person
    The right place
    The right time
And poof!
We reconnect
With our past
It is the lessons
The love we crave
    To complete a cycle
    To complete a love
The missing piece
The enhancement
    To a puzzle
We may have not known
We needed

Gypsy Mercer

<u>ALIVE</u>

I see your pulse racing
I feel your roaring thunder
My eyes open in expectation
You never disappoint
I come alive in your presence
I embrace our passion
I feed you my soul
Emptying me
As you fill me
With your love

WILD WOMAN 1

Her wild
Will drive you to distraction
Accountability is not a given
If you choose her
Do not anticipate taming her
She will decide
In her own time
What she can or will give
Without destroying herself

Gypsy Mercer

WILD WOMAN 2

A wild woman will find you
If you are worthy
If you tempt her curiosity
Or challenge her mind
Be sure to keep up
Lesser men have tried
And fallen into the abyss
With those lacking value
Lie, cheat, steal
And her fiery nature
Will mark your descent
Into oblivion

GOODBYE

They never ended
    The dreams
I replayed them
    Every night
They were the ruler
    I used to measure
        All things
The ruler always won
I once bid my dreams
    Goodbye
But they would not listen
Knowing my heart
    Spoke louder
Begging them
    To come alive

Gypsy Mercer

<u>HOPE</u>

The more I feel
    The less adequate my words
The deeper I go
    My words fail me
I am left with emotions
    That bounce off walls
        Not offering answers
When I say I love you
    I peel back layers
        Of fears and tears
Giving you virgin feelings
    Never shared with another
Filled with promise and hope
    And the essence of me

LOVING YOU

Sometimes the only gift
    Is closure
I did not intend to leave an open wound
Nor did I want you to feel pain
I share the blame
    In our broken relationship
I never meant to lease space
    In your dreams
        Your memories
But maybe I did
I let you homestead in mine
Comparing me to others was a mistake
The relationships did not go well
Giving up on love was a mistake
    I truly know
My heart could not break any more
    Than it has
Finally understanding
    What we were
    Who we are
How deeply we loved
How intertwined we still are
The wasted years with the wrong people
Loving you was no illusion
    It was magic

Gypsy Mercer

RARE

I write you upon my soul
I know your every refinement
    Your smell
    Your taste
    Your touch upon my heart
All with eyes that are closed
Feeling you in another dimension
    So intensely
You live within me
I know the depth of your eyes
    So filled with emotion
Dark hair that curls your toes
Your arms strong enough to hold me
To love and protect me
    From all but you
With open eyes
Will you still lie beside me
Or must I leave you
    In my heart

EMPTY

I have run out of love
Maybe we are given a limited supply
Maybe my urn is empty
Maybe I should have loved less
    Given less
    Felt less
    Saved it all for me
Maybe I was foolish
    And threw it all away
Maybe my heart had a hole in it
    And it drained
        Bit by bit
        Day by day
After we gave up
    On each other
    On ourselves
And the sky lost the sun

Gypsy Mercer

WOULD I

If I had a chance to do it again
    Would I
Would I do it exactly the same
    To relive the magical moments
Would I change things
    Hoping for a different ending
Would I be brave enough
    To reopen the door
    Or lock it and throw away the key
Would I run in the opposite direction
Would I walk into fire and flame
Would I care
Would I dare
Would it matter
Choice is not always a gift

THE YEARS

A lifetime of memories
    Of dreams
    Of maybes
    Of what ifs
Sadness

Gladness

Madness

Filled with laughter, love, lust
    Your smile
    Your kiss
    Your leaving
    My loss
The years

The tears

The fears
    All came too fast
    All came back to you

Gypsy Mercer

QUASARS

My love
I offer you
An anticipation more urgent than passion
An intoxication more heady than alcohol
A freedom more liberating than flight
A satisfaction deeper than imagination
A love more powerful than quasars
My love rekindled by fire
Fueled by urgency and fear
That one lifetime is insufficient
To house our cosmic soul connection
Take my hand
Follow me into the Black Hole
Of Time
Warping space into our own reality
Where we will love without restraint

HIJACKED

Some men hijack all your senses
Their smile is infectious
    Causing your lips to join the fun
Their eyes sparkle
    As though having a life of their own
Their laugh, their expressions
Send shivers up your spine
Their cologne
    Although intoxicating
Does not measure up to the aroma
    Of their maleness
Their tough
    Bold
    Confident
    Teasing
All because they are in your head
Reading your every nuance
    Feeling and living it with you

Gypsy Mercer

<u>LOVE AGAIN</u>

I saw you earlier today
You were laughing
    And smiling
        So handsome
        So happy
Letting you go was painful
And broke my heart
There was no greater gift
    I could give you
Than to let you
Love again
    Without me

DIMINISHED

My mind
Tells me to forget you
But it will be me
Who is diminished
When you are gone

Gypsy Mercer

REMEMBER

I want to remember
I hid so long
I forgot
    The electricity of your touch
    The taste of your kiss
    The ripple as you nuzzle my neck
    The warmth of your breath
    The fullness of your love
I have opened the gates
Please proceed gently
Then boldly
I want to remember
And feel it all

FLOW

Kiss me deeply
So my knees give way
So my words slur
So my eyes fall shut
So my skin tingles
And my emotions
    My motions
Flow within you
As our bodies melt
And merge as one

Gypsy Mercer

<u>CAMOUFLAGE</u>

I think I know you
    But I don't
Camouflages as love
Morphing into Adonis
The incubus of my dreams
Kissing me with promises
As you vaporize
Upon my touch
Yet tangible enough
To capture my heart
One breath at a time

LEAVES

Wicked

Wild

Watching

Season's change

The breeze in the trees

Nature's gift

Leaves aplenty

Crisp bright moons

Bring peace

And understanding

Gypsy Mercer

PROMISE

I could not save you
I tried
I had sheltered you
But could not protect you
From the same demons
I fought in the dark
I understand your pain
Your doubt
Your guilt
The inability to forget
But I can make this promise
One day
You will raise your head
Flip back your hair
Stand two inches taller
And remind the world
That you are a Warrior
That your Phoenix has risen
That you will not show
Mercy
To your attackers
This I promise you

OSMOSIS

I will not hide under a rock
Rather I will be in plain sight
Tempting your every sense
Until through osmosis
I permeate all your senses
And you feel me with every thought
Know me in every inch

Gypsy Mercer

INNUENDO

I praise innuendo
Starkness is too sharp
My mind craves gentle
But my soul embodies passion
In brilliant colors
Edges that keep you sharp
Depth that is boundless
Time that is eternal
And a net
To hold me securely
While I float in freedom

MORNING

I woke up this morning
And you were gone
Mornings are so lonely
Without you
Tangled sheets
Physical feats
Bring a smile to my face

Your silence is overwhelming
A void
Where laughter
And love
Should be

Let me unsay the words
That forced you to go
And vow the words
You want to hear
To bring you near

Gypsy Mercer

<u>GALAXIES</u>

It is in the safety of my love
You thrive
I give you unconditional love
As a platform
To reach the galaxies
Retreating into my bosom
When needed
Rising when desired
Your safe haven
Gifted from me to you

Virgo Unbound

MY SOUL

My heart is young
But my soul is old
I love madly and deeply
But my soul knows the cost
My heart craves love to survive
My soul remembers it well and is sad
My mind is agile
But my body is tired
How can so much be given
Then taken
When I need it most

Gypsy Mercer

<u>BEAST</u>

...because I am the good girl
that can tame the beast...

DREAMING

...dreaming you into my life
into my reality...

Gypsy Mercer

<u>THE SEA</u>

The soothing fire
Its comforting warmth
The rhythm of the sea
Serenading me
The star filled night
Illuminating the sky
And you beside me
Ecstasy

CATACOMBS

Catacombs
Filled with empty spaces
For memories
Not destined to be forgotten
To be revisited
When the soul needs solace
Recovering the emotion
Needed
To continue
Enabling the hearts
Perilous journey
And joyous delight

Gypsy Mercer

FOREVER AND A DAY

Soulmates branded

In the now and forever

Loudly quiet

Quietly strong

One look

    One kiss

        One touch

            One thought

Sends my heart on a race

Only meant for the fleet footed

On a path leading to you

So mismatched

Yet so perfect

The snap of completion

You and me

Together

Forever

    And a day

LOVE ME

I wanted you to know
I love you
But I cannot stay
To be the love
I feel you deserve
I must be perfect
I am not
I am flawed
I cannot bear
Disappointing you
Or destroying me
My parting wish
For you
Is a perfect love
I wish it were me

Gypsy Mercer

SMILE AGAIN

I had forgotten
It happened over time
It was gone
Before I recognized it
We parted
Brave faces all around
My smile went the way of
Fairytales and fantasies
Dreams and wishes
I want to smile again
Teach me how
Let me believe again

LATE

She holds on to you
Like you are the last straw
While drowning in quicksand
You still drink the air
Unaware
She tried
Offering you her best
Too late
To change fate
You had moved on

Gypsy Mercer

MADNESS

He created a madness in her
He could not control
What started as delectation
Turned to sorrow
As he watched her burn

RUSHING

Rushing
Getting nowhere fast
Pedal on the gas
    To make the dash
Trying to catch a dream
Fading from memory
Making it a reality
Before the crash
Into the ghost garden
For eternity

Gypsy Mercer

MY FRIEND

I forgot
How to feel
I knew the words
But the feelings
Escaped me
They had been shelved
Years ago
Because their pain
Was too intense
You slid in
With your darkness
And brought me back to life
I dug deep to share your pain
Hoping to diminish it
I held your hand
While you tumbled my walls
Making me whole again
And vulnerable
With you
And stronger
Beside you

OTHERWORLDLY

Reaching for you

Touching you

Feeling you

Feeling me

Touching me

Creates

Otherworldly emotions

Within me

Beyond the

Here and now

That only dreams

Dare to express

Gypsy Mercer

INFINITE

You are mine
I name you
I claim you
You live in my heart
My thoughts
I awake with you beside me
Laughing and loving me
Messed hair
Sleepy eyes
That is both of us
Smiles our only cover
I pledge my love to you
With each breath
We are made whole
And infinite

Virgo Unbound

MY PATH

Some days my path is clear
Other days shielded by smoke
And mirrors
Distorted yet clear
Testing my resolve
Tempting me to explore
Another fork in the road
Already riddled with
Broken puzzle pieces
Tried and discarded
Because they did not fit
Despite the effort

Gypsy Mercer

NO QUESTIONS

No questions

I am here

That is answer enough

Your pull

I cannot resist

My heart will not listen

Nor does it want to

What I feel

In your presence

Transcends

All that is good in the world

And tantalizes

All that is bad

Chaos rules my heart

Your touch sets me free

Enjoying a bliss

Only you can share

REMEMBERING

The rhythm is hypnotic
Following your lead
Is so natural
Your cologne brings back
Memories
The whispers
The touch
Breaks my heart
As I remember him

Gypsy Mercer

LIES

Lies do not disappear
They continue to haunt
Eroding the foundation
Of every belief
Until it crumbles
From deceit
Leaving only the pain
In its wake

UNTIL YOU

Not lonely
Incomplete
Until you

Missing pieces
Dusty on shelves
Forgotten
Until you

Not broken
Not recognized
Not needed
Until you

Now whole
Because of you

Gypsy Mercer

NAME

And just like that

You sat down next to me

Knowing it was your place

Your face unfamiliar

But your soul sang to me

Your smile

Yes

Your smile

Will be the life of me

You ordered for two

As I knew you would

Turning to me

You said

Hello

My name is...

US

Our secret

Our time

We are two souls

Destined to unite

But the time

Is not right

WE feel

We understand

Without reason

Believing we are insane

Yet knowing

Deep within

There is but one

Outcome

Us

Gypsy Mercer

APEX

Rise above mediocrity
Pave your own path
As you soar to the apex
As it was meant to be

Virgo Unbound

<u>THE SKY</u>

When the sun leaves the sky
And your insecurities
Give rise to melancholy
Reach for me
I cannot give you strength
But I can share mine
I will hold your hand
So you do not blink from the glare
When the sky cries
I will shelter you from the storm
I will catch you
As lightening takes your breath
And thunder leaves you shaken
I will always be there

Gypsy Mercer

<u>CONFUSED</u>

My color is confused
Not purple, blue or red
Maybe plaid
I know not what you say
Using our words
To mean different things
The witching hour comes
When puzzle pieces snap together
My hello can be your goodbye
Your later may mean never
Until the moment
Our souls speak
Our forgotten language
Meant only for two

TO THE MOON

They stood atop a ridge

One star studded night

Breeze tickling their fur

Taking turns

Howling soulful solos

To the moon

Each howl deeper

Than the last

Feeling empowered

As the moon answered back

And their dominance

Was assured

Gypsy Mercer

DISTANCE

I distance myself
From deep feelings
Do not want the pain
From letting go
I cheat myself of joy
Never allowing it in
A price I am willing to pay
Breaking from the inside out
Is a weakness
I will not accept
Rebuilding is not an option
I have already closed the door
To healing
To love

POWER

Power is one stroke
Not a mass of little ones
Finality its score

Gypsy Mercer

WARP

Do not warp my reality
I have no time for games
I stopped playing with boys
A long time ago
It takes a real man
To capture my attention
And a strong man
To hold it

TAME

...I promise
    not to tame you...
Your wild sets me free

Gypsy Mercer

GAMES

You lit my fuse
Now you are fuel to my fire
You thought I was down
For the count
I play to win
I am a Past Master
Time to take out my arsenal
It has been resting for years
Though dusty and rusty
My blood boiling brings it
Back to life
You lose
You will not see me coming
Yet your body will shudder
From the force you feel
But do not see
Vengeance is in the air

Virgo Unbound

Never ever get between me and mine
Your power play went flat
Time to rethink
Your battle strategy
I have only just begun
Your mediocre games
Do little except
Strengthen my resolve
You thought my Warrior
Was but a myth
Welcome to my playground
Winning is my goal
Cost is inconsequential
There will be no hostages
Nor any prisoners
Let the games begin

Gypsy Mercer

ASSUMPTIONS

Do not assume

I am like the others

Or that they are like me

They are incapable

Of knowing you as I do

We stop time

Languish within each other's soul

Speak our own language

Breathe each other's breath

Face each other's fears

Consume each other's joy

Because we begin

Where the other ends

CONSUMING

Do not try to make me
Someone I am not
I am not lukewarm
Nor clay you can mold
I am fire
With flames of blue
Hypnotic
Demanding
Consuming
And I come for you

Gypsy Mercer

IT IS TIME

It is time
To let you go
Once attentive
    Now cavalier
Words were promises
    Not possibilities
Kisses were bold
    Not lackluster
Love was automatic
    Not stages
I long for abandon
Time without end
Electrical connection
Just no longer with you
Our spark died long ago

MISSTEPS

It is our turn
We have made our mistakes
Taken wrong turns
We have no time to waste
No more foolish pride
We will meet in the middle
Forgive and forget
Start anew
Pledge our honor
To love one another
To move forward without fear

Gypsy Mercer

<u>SECOND THOUGHTS</u>

Waiting

Not my strong suit

Finger tapping

Legs swinging

You are late

    Late like not early

    Late like not here yet

Imagining disasters

Second thoughts

Forgotten promises

I hear your brakes squeal

Car door slams

Bold knock

Now all is right

In my world

SHE SEES HIM

He sees you
Really sees you
Questions and doubts
Will this time be different
What can I do
To ensure he stays
This time
My heart still bruised
My confidence at a standstill
Can I keep him
Long enough
That he will want to stay
And never run away

Gypsy Mercer

YEARS

You are hesitant
To let her in
She left you
All those years ago
Will she stay this time
Is she the same soul
Who captured your heart
And imagination
In your youthful bliss
Is she still fire
And passion
Will the torch rekindle
Will she quench your thirst
Will she bring peace
To all your tomorrows

OPEN DOOR

The years
The tears
Now you
The door is open once more
Hesitant
Wary
Your pull is intense
I have no choice
But to follow
Or cast myself into oblivion
In a void without you
Fearful each volley
Will be the last
I act and react by instinct
Dreaming of a future
Long overdue

Gypsy Mercer

<u>FADING</u>

I thought I had time
I was used to settling
Weeks and months raced by
I was deteriorating
I accepted loss
As my expectations
Diminished
My heart shrank
Fading to a pale pink
The beating grew slower
As I became another
Ghost from your past

MULTIPLY

I am not diminished
Beside you
I know my worth
I know our strength together
We rule the universe
The world we created
Together we are unstoppable
We are united in our goals
We fill each other's weaknesses
We multiply our dominance
We are warriors
We are soulmates

Gypsy Mercer

MOONLIGHT

The sky so black
The shimmering moon
Suspended in the northern sky
Our naked vulnerability
Our strength growing
By the hour
As dreams
And promises
Whispered by moonlight
Become animated
As the sun
Sets our world on fire
Releasing us
Once more

REALITY

We should give us a chance
To finally know
If memories
    Hopes
    Dreams
Were strong enough
To pull the best of us
From yesterday's ghosts
No more aborted tries
Let this be our last stand
Our encore
To finally know
Truth from fantasy
Our new reality

Gypsy Mercer

FREEDOM

You fell in love
With a taste of freedom
Pulsing through your soul
Little did you know
Freedom would be your undoing
To capture a butterfly
Requires patience
    Planning
    Commitment
She had no time for sightseers
Who looked to add to their collection
    Suspended
    Without flight
And you would not
Offer your freedom
To capture hers

SIMPLE TRUTH

Simple truth

I love you

Always will

But I do not want to hurt

Anymore

It used to be easy

We let fears

Turn to tears

Breaking our hearts

Once again

Together

Praying we get it right

This time

Gypsy Mercer

INSTINCT

I rely on instinct
On intuition
Both have served me well
I discount stories
Unless they are my own
I feel emotions
I see truth
I trust in myself
I rarely am mistaken
Should I be
I alone will pay the price

Virgo Unbound

CLOSED DOORS

Your passion is boundless
As is your artic freeze
I believe the heat scares you
Then you lock the doors
Only to reopen
When the fear subsides
Leaving me confused
Yet hopeful
My caution builds
With each closure
Knowing you truly love me
Hurts the most

Gypsy Mercer

<u>RAPTURE</u>

You awakened my wild
Reminding me of those things
I cannot do without
I am a force felt on so many levels
A demand that cannot be denied
I am visionary
    I see beyond the mundane
I succor and protect
    That which is mine
    By right or divine gift
I am rapture
I must be appeased

MY STORM

You were not strong enough

To enter my storm

You like safe

I am not

I run with wolves

And leave behind

The weak or indecisive

I invited you into my world

The waters are deep

And the fire burns

You are welcome to

Your mediocrity

And unfulfilled dreams

You have no place in mine

Gypsy Mercer

Who is Gypsy Mercer?

She is a girl that turned into a woman who read poetry and believed in Knights and magic.

Gypsy began writing in college when she found that her thoughts and written prose were so much more powerful than speaking the words.

Life and reality forced a hiatus while she raised a family and made her way into the professional world. All along, she believed that her real world was in opposition to the needs of her heart and her soul. No longer constrained, she picked up her pen freeing both.

This is the result of her escape from captivity into creativity.

Follow Gypsy Mercer
www.GypsyMercer.com
Facebook: GypsySong
Instagram: @MercerGypsy

www.ingramcontent.com/pod-product-compliance
Lightning Source LLC
Chambersburg PA
CBHW070549050426
42450CB00011B/2784